Saint Valentine

The Patron Saint of Love

Find our books at Amazon, Barnes & Nobles, Walmart, Books-A-Million, OverDrive, Kobo, Lulu and more!

Like, Share and Follow us on Facebook, Instagram, Twitter, Pinterest, YouTube, LinkedIn, Spotify, Apple Podcast and more!

www.SlothDreamsBooks.com

www.SlothDreamsBooks.com

Published by Sloth Dreams Books & Publishing LLC.
Sloth Dreams Children's Books
Pennsylvania, USA
www.SlothDreamsBooks.com

Saint Valentine

The Patron Saint of Love

Written & Illustrated
by KeriAnne Jelinek

Once upon a time, a long time ago, there was a kind and caring man named Saint Valentine. He was born in the 3rd century AD. He was from the country of Italy. There are many unknown facts about St. Valentine and his childhood.

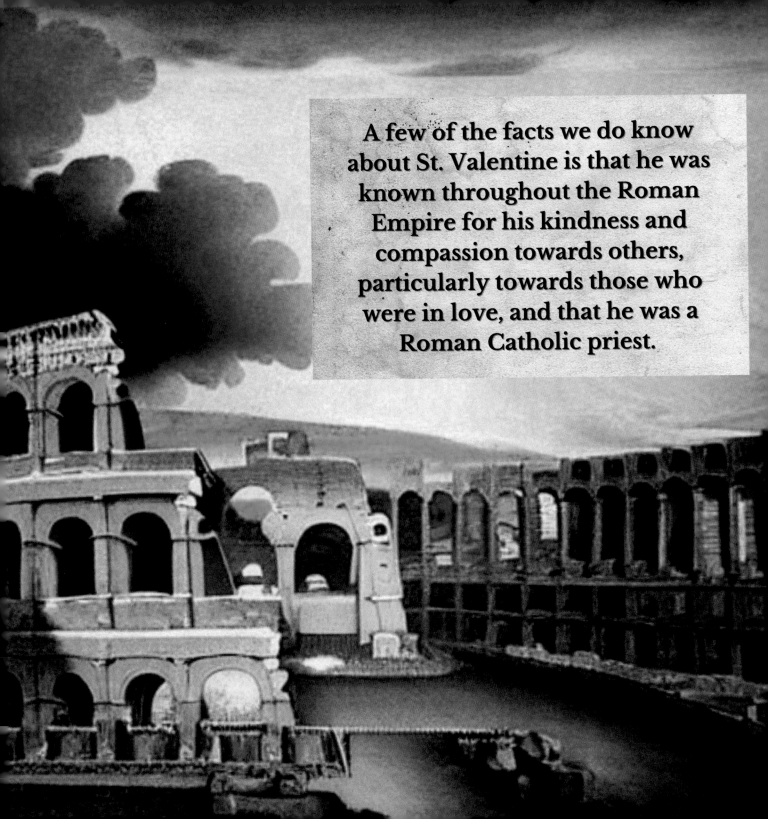

A few of the facts we do know about St. Valentine is that he was known throughout the Roman Empire for his kindness and compassion towards others, particularly towards those who were in love, and that he was a Roman Catholic priest.

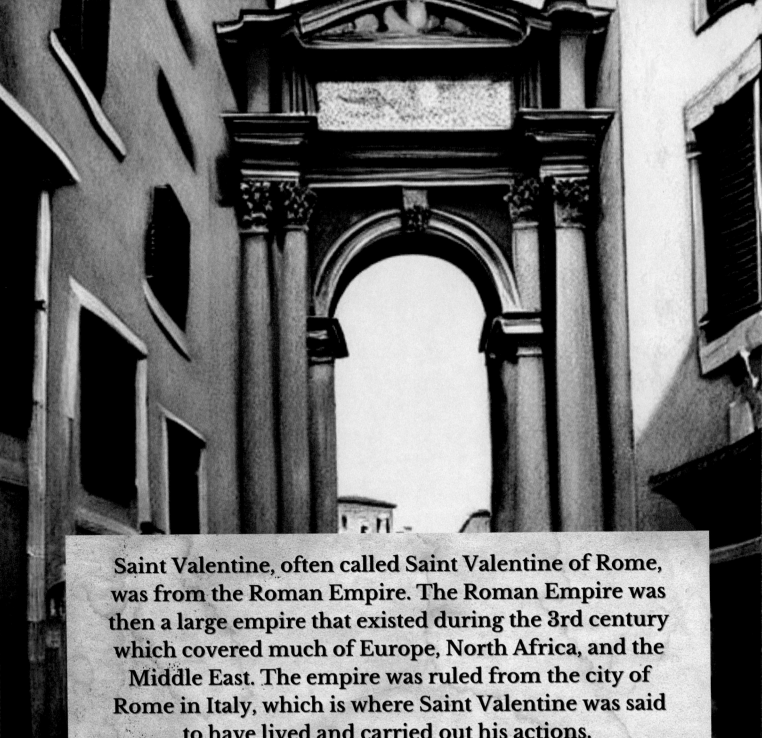

Saint Valentine, often called Saint Valentine of Rome,
was from the Roman Empire. The Roman Empire was
then a large empire that existed during the 3rd century
which covered much of Europe, North Africa, and the
Middle East. The empire was ruled from the city of
Rome in Italy, which is where Saint Valentine was said
to have lived and carried out his actions.

During this time, there were many different accounts of men named St. Valentine. Since there are several Saint Valentines', it's not clear which of them is being referred to when talking about the Saint Valentine of Rome, as they all lived in different parts of the Roman Empire, and all their stories were not well-documented.

At the time, the Roman Empire was in power, and the emperor, Claudius II, had banned marriages because he believed that unmarried men made better soldiers. Claudius believed soldiers would be distracted from their work if they were married.

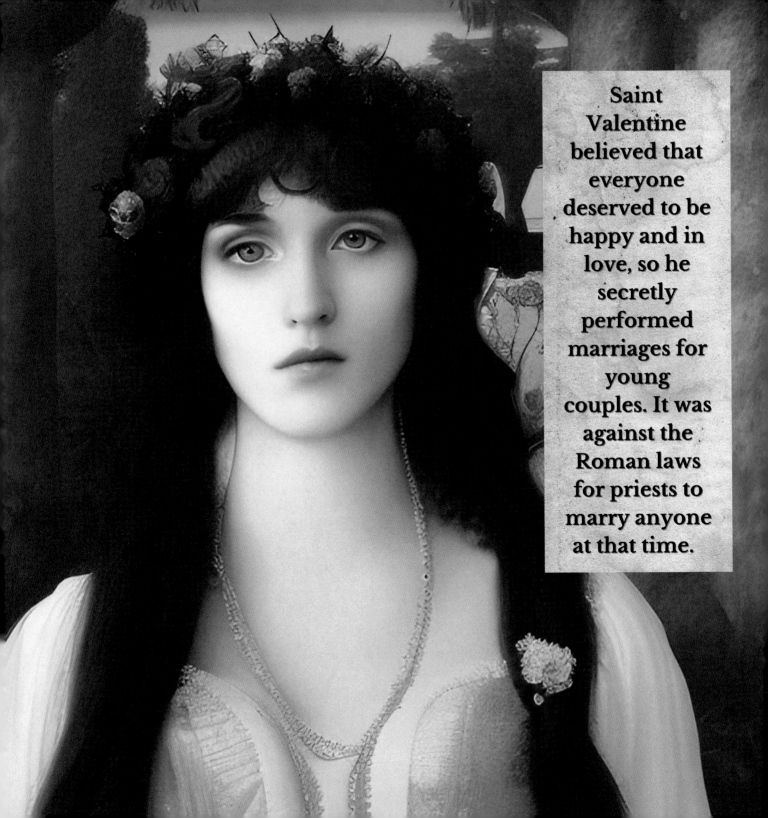

Saint Valentine believed that everyone deserved to be happy and in love, so he secretly performed marriages for young couples. It was against the Roman laws for priests to marry anyone at that time.

One day, the emperor found out about Saint Valentine's actions, and he was very angry. The emperor ordered Saint Valentine to be arrested and thrown into prison. While Saint Valentine was in prison, he continued to help and comfort the other prisoners. He even helped heal the sick and injured.

Claudius II ordered for St. Valentine to be killed for not obeying his law. Before Saint Valentine was put to death, he sent a letter to a young girl who he had become friends with while in prison. This letter was the first known "Valentine's Day" letter ever written. In the letter, Saint Valentine wrote about the power of love and how it can overcome even the darkest of situations.

On February 14th, 270 AD, Saint Valentine was put to death for his actions. But his memory lived on, and people began to honor him by celebrating Saint Valentine's life and the message of love and kindness by exchanging cards, flowers, and gifts on February 14th, which is now known as Valentine's Day.

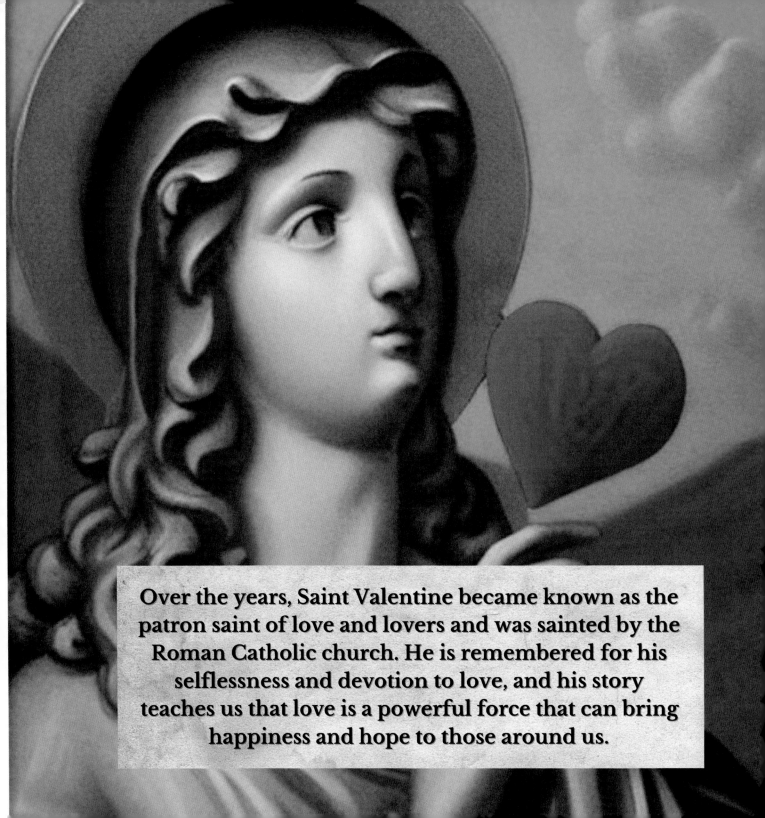

Over the years, Saint Valentine became known as the patron saint of love and lovers and was sainted by the Roman Catholic church. He is remembered for his selflessness and devotion to love, and his story teaches us that love is a powerful force that can bring happiness and hope to those around us.

Saint Valentine is remembered as a true
romantic hero and a symbol of love, devotion,
and selflessness. His story teaches us that love
is a powerful force that can bring hope
and happiness to those around us.

Made in the USA
Coppell, TX
09 February 2023

12431755R00019